Additional praise for the *Tiny Book of Thoughts* series

"*Tiny thoughts - - tiny but profound is all I can say! Very, very inspiring!*"
- **Lauren MacLauclan**, author of *The Law of Attraction 'How–to' Book'*.

"*Small books with big wisdom.*"
- **Peace Pilgrim II,** renown peace advocate and author of *Enjoying the Journey*.

"*Thank you so much for your wonderful books – your quotes are marvelous and our readers will love them…Your Thoughts and energy are deeply appreciated.*"
- **Lee Simonson**, Publisher of *Heartwarmers* and *Petwarmers*.

"*I really enjoyed reading and reflecting on your short and sweet, actionable and inspiring thoughts. They get to the heart of the matter for deep learning from within.*"
- **Jengiz Gocer** – Business Consultant and facilitator for the *Learner Within* ™ *Box*.

"*A wonderful collection of introspective and inspiring thoughts that can change your life.*"
- **L. Fownes**

MORE TINY THOUGHTS FOR PERSONAL TRANSFORMATION

Also by Karl Schmidt

Tiny Thoughts for Personal Transformation
©2013   ISBN: 978-0-9686831-3-2 (pbk.)

Another Tiny Book of Thoughts
©2003   ISBN: 0-9686831-2-6

A Tiny Book of Thoughts Too
©2001   ISBN: 0-9686831-1-8

A Tiny Book of Thoughts
©2000   ISBN: 0-9686831-0-x

The *Tiny Books* each contain just over 70 aphorisms/thoughts, many of which are found in this book, and the books themselves are physically small (3"x5"). These books were self-published and were not widely distributed; consequently, if you want more information about them, or if you wish to purchase one of the few remaining copies, please visit me at:

www.TinyThoughtGuy.com

MORE TINY THOUGHTS FOR PERSONAL TRANSFORMATION

change your thoughts, change your life

Karl Schmidt

Inspired Crow
Publications

The necessary legal stuff

Published in Canada by Inspired Crow Publications

Cover design and photography by Karl Schmidt

Library and Archives Canada Cataloguing in Publication

Schmidt, Karl, 1968-, author
    More tiny thoughts for personal transformation : change your thoughts, change your life / Karl Schmidt.

 Issued in print and electronic formats.
 ISBN 978-0-9686831-7-0 (pbk.).--
 ISBN 978-0-9686831-8-7 (pdf).--
 ISBN 978-0-9686831-9-4 (mobi).--
 ISBN 978-1-987845-00-6 (epub)

        1. Aphorisms and apothegms. 2. Self-actualization (Psychology).
 I. Title.

 PN6271.S354 2015   158.1   C2014-907985-0
                                      C2014-907986-9

Dedication
- In Gratitude -

I am a firm believer that in order to grow, just like everything else in nature, we need three things: a foundation, energy/light, and nutrients.

My Foundation

These are the people that were there from the very beginning and, although some of them have since transitioned to the next part of their journey, I am forever grateful to them for giving me the foundation, the initial tools that were so crucial for the start of my journey. Without the tools and care given to me by these people I would not have had the foundation to build upon and after floating around aimlessly I would have likely wandered off course. For their gifts and guidance I give heartfelt thanks to: Mom, Dad, Oma, Karl, the Universal Force and Gaia.

My Light Bringers

These are the individuals with whom I have shared a portion of my journey and who have positively enriched me with their essence and presence. Although my intention is to express my gratitude to each and every person that fits into this category, there probably are not enough pages in this book, so I will simply say that I appreciate all you have done for me and you are forever part of my experience. You have my eternal gratitude and I wish all of you unbounded happiness.

My Nutritionists

This section could also have been titled, "My Manure Bringers", or even, "My ….(oh, I guess I'm not allowed to use that phrase=;0). As with the previous section, there are a vast number of people that I could include here, but you didn't honestly expect me to give you a list did you? In all seriousness though, there are a great number of people with whom I have interacted where the experience might not be labeled as "pleasant." This does not mean however that the experience was any less valuable than those experiences that I would label as joyous or pleasant. It is my firm belief that there are two main types of experiences in life: those we enjoy, and those that force us to grow. In many ways, the experiences that we consider unpleasant or that are associated with our greatest obstacles are often the precise experiences we need to propel us forward. To all of the people on this list I express my gratitude for helping me to learn some of the most important lessons on my journey thus far and for tolerating my lack of awareness. **Namaste**.

"Our achievements of today are but the sum total of our thoughts of yesterday. You are today where the thoughts of yesterday have brought you and you will be tomorrow where the thoughts of today take you."
-Blaise Pascal

WARNING

Just like the waistband on a cheap pair of underwear that does not go back to its original form after it has been stretched by one too many desserts, so too is the mind unable to contract after being exposed to new ideas. If you decide to read this book, or even if you just open it up and read a single thought, your mind will be altered forever. Perhaps by reading this book your life will be enriched, perhaps not. Perhaps you will agree with some of the information on the following pages, or perhaps some of the information will irritate you. Perhaps the meaning behind some of the aphorisms will be blatantly clear and obvious to you, or perhaps you will find some of them vague and confusing. With this book **I only make one guarantee and that is: after reading any, some, or all of the information contained herein, your life will never be the same**. Just by the mere fact that you have read this, your life is impacted. I believe that, "***Experience is a process, not an event***" so ANYTHING and EVERYTHING that we come into conscious contact with will forever alter our consciousness and therefore, it is extremely important that we selectively choose what content we allow into our minds. With this book my intention is to - share some thoughts/aphorisms that will add to your journey in a positive manner: I believe they will. At this point I should also mention how I define an "aphorism." I see an aphorism as a brief or short saying that embodies a general truth or observation. Certainly some debate can be had as to what is merely a thought and what is an aphorism; I don't want to enter into that debate here. My desire is to share some ideas, concepts, thoughts or aphorisms, whatever label you choose to use, that have been part of my journey and my truth. I will share more in a moment about how I see "My Truth" in relation to "The Truth."

Well, that's it. That's the warning message. If you have made it this far, you might as well read the actual introduction.

**Please note that this text and the images in this book are deliberately large in size to assist those with visual impairments.

INTRODUCTION

Greetings. and "Thank you" for taking the time to read the introduction. While this section is almost identical to the introduction in the previous book, *Tiny Thoughts for Personal Transformation*, I thought it would be beneficial to re-state the information because my desire in sharing these thoughts/aphorisms has remained the same and there might be readers who are not familiar with my intent.

This introduction is a key component to understanding what it is that I am trying to do with all of this ink on paper (or if you are reading this on an electronic device, with all of these zeros and ones). I must admit, my own tendency in the past was to usually skip the introduction of a book and get right into the main content. Certainly there are times when this works just fine, but there are other times when the introduction is actually a key component that prepares the reader for the content. In a way I guess it is similar to fast forwarding a movie to the "good parts" and not "wasting time" with the "other stuff." Although one can still enjoy a movie by watching it this way, a great deal is lost in the process.

With a book like this, and by "this" I mean a book with small bites of information and

no explanation, **I believe that it is important to understand the essence of what I'm doing in order for you to get the full benefit of the material**. Because, (weren't we always told in school never to start a sentence with the word "because?") **the aphorisms and thoughts contained on these pages are very concentrated,** I consider this book to be the "advanced course." As such, the reader is left to ponder these aphorisms on their own and I do not provide any personal opinions as to what I believe they mean. I did not include any analysis or opinion, not to frustrate the reader or to be aloof; rather, I believe that it is important for the reader to expand their awareness through the process of contemplation, rather than by simply reading a concept and then having me give my "biased" opinion. This is to say that while there is "The Truth" the only thing that we are actually capable of sharing is "Our Truth", a subset of "The Truth" that has been influenced by our experiences and perceptions. We are unique in an infinite number of ways and, as a result, our truth cannot be somebody else's truth. Our uniqueness is an amazing gift that is helping us to create our reality for this journey, so for us to impose "Our Truth" is counterproductive to everyone. Furthermore, I remember some of the textbooks from school that had the answers at the back of the book. Of course, I would never just skip to the back of the book and read the answer, but I hear that some people did =;0) Okay, I confess, I did that on occasion; however, as is often the case in life, I gave the answer that somebody, in this case the teacher, wanted to hear, and then I failed the test miserably. By simply regurgitating information, by not putting in the effort ourselves, we might acquire knowledge and we might be able to impress people, yet when it truly comes to understanding something, when it comes to gaining wisdom, the truth is revealed and we are lacking.

In this book I share "My Truth" and I offer it only as a means for you to see reality from a different perspective. The aphorisms/thoughts contained on these pages were derived from meditations and moments of Satori (a Zen term for awareness or awakening). I believe that the aphorisms came through me and I was merely the scribe who recorded them. These aphorisms were pertinent to my journey at a specific time in my life, yet it seems that as life progresses they remain part of my truth. It is not my intention to give advice nor to make claims that my experiences will in any way impact your life.

To illustrate this point, when I originally put pen to paper, for those old enough to remember paper (wink, wink), a friend read over what I had been writing and said to me, "Just like that old adage, it sounds like you want to show people how to fish, rather than simply give them a fish." I mulled over that statement and, trying not to be disrespectful, went on to say that, "To me it is even more than that: my desire is simply to go fishing and to allow others to watch me fish. If there is something that I do that allows them to be better at fishing, then that is superb. On the other hand, if what I am doing does not improve what they are already doing then I do not want to impose my way of fishing on them. They should continue to do as they have been doing."

It is also important to mention that **if something in this book touches you or inspires you, that's fantastic, but realize that this book was only a spark. Any changes you make were already within you and can only be accredited to you: changes only come from within**. It may take time, but I truly believe that anything we do that brings more light into the world is a positive thing. Conversely, in the event that some of the information contained on these pages does not ring true for you, PLEASE leave that thought/concept behind and move on to another one.

Indeed, even in my own experience there were concepts that I initially rejected. On one occasion I remember reading an aphorism after my meditation (many times when I wrote down thoughts I would not know what I wrote until later on when I re-read them) and thinking to myself, "This is nonsense, I don't believe that at all." I crumpled up the paper and I threw the note into the garbage bin (recycling wasn't as well-known back then). Later in the day (I assume my subconscious mind had been playing with the aforementioned thought) it hit me what the thought actually meant: all of a sudden I could relate to it. I went back to the garbage, which, thankfully, wasn't full of messy, gooey stuff, and pulled out the crumpled piece of paper. For me, this is what I would term an "A-ha" moment, or, as I mentioned earlier, "Satori." So, even if an idea does not resonate with you right away, let it go, and move on. Perhaps later in the day, or even many years later, it will resonate with you. We all know that the world was flat until 1522, there were no such things as germs until the 1860's, no human will ever walk on the moon, no human will ever run a mile in less than four minutes... As I said in the warning, when we are exposed to new ideas we can't help but be challenged by them and changed by them: each of us differently.

To that end, because we all learn in our own unique way and we all resonate with different ideas, I thought it would be appropriate to retain aphorisms that might have a similar theme.

Where possible, I have added an image or graphic for those who enjoy visual cues. In some cases the graphic might relate to the aphorism/thought in a literal sense, in other cases the connection may be more subtle.

I'm hoping that some of the graphics and some of the words on the following pages will present you with your own "A-ha" moments and maybe some of the aphorisms will allow you to see your world through new eyes. My job, my journey, is simply to share the thoughts and to allow the reader to do with them as they wish; however, to get the most out of our time together I would suggest that going slowly is the best way to take this journey. Perhaps take a thought a day or a few thoughts at a time and contemplate them. With the *Tiny Book of Thoughts* trilogy, some people shared that they would like to concentrate on a situation in their life and then randomly open the pages. In some cases the thought would give them an insight into their situation, perhaps a new way of seeing a relationship or a problem. If the idea on that particular page couldn't be directly related to their specific situation then the benefit was that they could use it to take their mind off their particular issue: I call this a "Pattern interrupt." That is to say that sometimes, when we get stuck in a thought spiral, we need something to interrupt that pattern, something to "get our mind off of" a particular issue so that we can think about it from a better head-space.

When you read a thought/aphorism you might contemplate what the aphorism means to you. Do you agree with what the thought infers, or do you disagree with what it says? Can the aphorism be used to improve the quality of your thinking or the quality of your relationships? However you choose to use the aphorisms is correct, I would only suggest that racing through the material will limit its usefulness. Many ideas come to us and we simply dismiss them by saying to ourselves, "I know that already." In some cases we do understand the idea and we have incorporated it into our lives: that's fantastic. In many instances though, we say that we "know" something when in actual fact we mean that we have "heard that before" or we "get it" on a surface level, not truly understanding it. We might know that a stove can be hot, but until we burn ourselves we don't truly understand what that means. We might "know" a word in a foreign language without actually being able to use or apply it. We might "know" how to ride a bike, but if we haven't ridden one in a while we will fall off a few times. Some of us "know" that certain foods don't react well with us, but it isn't until a little while later that our body reminds us, why we should not eat that food. So, remember that there is no need or benefit to rush through this meal, it's a big course and I believe you'll enjoy it more by taking your time: savor it. Please do not be fooled by the simplicity of many of these aphorisms: they are deliberately direct and to the point, they are not meant to be lengthy and wordy. The *Tao Te Ching* is considered by many to be one of the most amazing and powerful books ever written, yet there are only 81 very short sections (paragraphs). I am not saying that the information in this book is comparable to the Tao, I am saying that we should not use verboseness as a measure of effectiveness or importance.

On another note, you might notice that several of the words have been spelled in a manner that appears incorrect; however, this spelling was intentional and these are not typos.

Finally, I wish to thank you for your patience in reading this introduction and I will leave you to your thoughts.

I would rather
have a heart
that bleeds
than a heart
that chips.

Our
"imperfections"
are
what make us
uniquely perfect.

Chaos
is the energetic state
that fuels our movement
from stagnation
to exploration.

I appreciate
all of your presents,
yet it is your
presence
that is most
appreciated.

The conscious mind
doesn't know
what's needed
for the soul to grow.

5 Priceless treasures
that you can have for free
to make life GREAT:

Gratitude

Reverence

Enthusiasm

Authenticity

Trust

Science

is the process of

trying to fit

the infinite

into the

finite.

SPEED
LIMIT
∞

The party is over
and, as always,
Shoulda,
Coulda
and Woulda
arrived a moment
too late.

Greatness doesn't
come to those who
say what they do;
greatness comes
to those who
do what they say.

When giving,
do we give to those
who deserve,
or to those
who need?

Intention =
desire in motion.

Because of the clouds
a sunrise
is made even more
beautiful.

Opportunity
exists only
in the
moment.

Seek out
your greatest weakness,
acknowledge him
and befriend him,
for in so doing
you will find
that he is one of
your greatest
allies.

When we want to see
we open our eyes,
when we want to hear
we open our ears,
when we want to know,
we open our
hearts.

Hey dude,
your ripples
are distorting
my reflection.

My opinion
of you
doesn't change
who you are.

If you
break life
down into
dollars and cents,
you will always
be
shortchanged.

When we drink
in the beauty
of the universe
we realize that
the cup is always
full.

With our words
we can only preach;
in the end,
it is our actions
that teach.

G

N   I

I   V

Sarcasm
and cynicism
are the children
born of doubt
and raised by defeat.

The
unplanted seed
grows
no roots.

If time
is relative
then forever
depends
on how old
you are.

Knowledge
is pain;
wisdom
is happiness.

I would be grateful
if you would
keep your dogma
away from
my karma.

It's not a matter of
right or wrong,
it's a matter of
efficient or inefficient.

Necessity
may be
the mother of invention,
but experience
is the mother of wisdom.

Where does
"here" end
and "*there*"
begin?

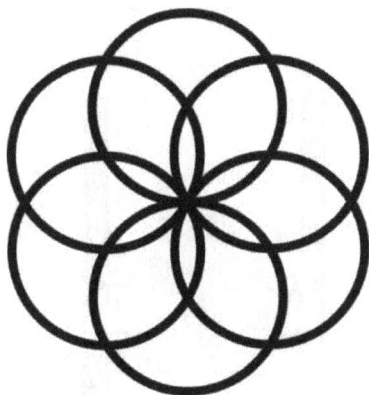

The Human
Experience
is the gap
between the doors
of infinity.

Bitterness:

cyanide

for the soul.

Even the most skilled
mechanic cannot
repair a vehicle
while it is in motion,
and aren't we all
the mechanics
of our own mind?

I'd rather live
as the exception.

Selfless and caring
thoughts are truly fine,
yet it is only
through action
that they become
divine.

Eagle or seagull,
the choice is yours:
either you go out
and get it for yourself,
or you get somebody
else's leftovers.

The answers
to many of life's
questions
have been written
on the
insides of our eyelids.

Thanksgiving Day
takes place
on one day of the year,
but giving thanks
is best done
every day
of the year.

Fear of death
is not fear of the unknown...
fear of death
is the fear
that you have to give
up all of the things
you THINK you own.

Imitation
might be flattering,
but it certainly is
not furthering.

Even

when the ship is sinking

there are those

who still insist

that nobody rocks

the boat.

Unless
you're a nudist,
you'll die with clothes
in your hamper.

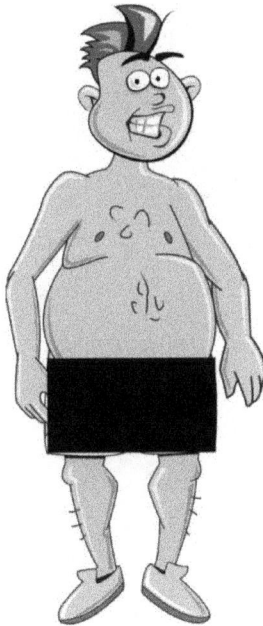

P-revious
A-ctions
S-tealing
T-ime

In order to recover
from defeat,
you need to move
de-feet.

The movement
to greater harmony
is always the result of one
loving and brave soul
who refuses to stay grounded
in what is and,
instead,
grows wings
to rise above
and lift others
to where they can see
the divine view
for themselves.

To merely memorize
is to be
mesmerized.

If the road to hell
is paved with
good intentions,
then you missed
the turn off.

NO, YOU WERE SUPPOSED TO TURN <u>LEFT</u> AT KINDNESS CRESCENT.

It's ironic
that those
who are quick
to forgive others
can often be slow
to forgive themselves.

In order for me
to be this,
I had to be
that.

Every journey
begins
by getting off your
if'n *but*.

The words within
a book
only provide
the information,
it is up to you
to choose
their application.

Perhaps we can't control
what images (thoughts)
flash onto
the movie screen
of the mind,
yet we do control
how many times
we hit the
rewind button.

To be,
or not to be,
that ...
is up to you.

If it is raining,
and I love you,
it's still raining.

If I love you,
and it's raining,
I still love you.

Just as
you are entitled
to be "right,"
so too
are others entitled
to be "wrong."

Sadness
is brought on
when we perceive
a gap
between where we are
and where we <u>think</u>
we should be.

Flowers
bloom
for
whom?

You need
all the time you have,
but you have
all the time you need.

The light
itself
does not dim,
it only appears so
as one moves
farther away.

If you truly wish
to show that you care,
merely WAKE UP
and become aware.

It is often
impossible to see
what we are doing
to others
until someone
does it to
us.

Elusive is happiness
when we pursue,
but do what you love
and it comes to you.

Error
lies
only in
interpretation.

True genius
is the ability to swim
against
the gray undercurrents
of mediocrity.

Love
is what remains
when the illusions
of separateness
dissolve.

By choosing
to be of service
to others
we ensure that
the spark of
humanity residing
within us
remains
constantly aglow.

Who
lives by the
clock
dies by the
clock.

What is,
always was;
what isn't,
never was.

One
who waits
to hear the applause
may never
get a chance
to give
an encore.

I believe,
yet sometimes
I forget.

Often
the people
that need help
the most
are least likely
to accept it.

I never
want to own
anything
that owns
me.

Even though
we may not see
the tree
of our good deeds
blossom,
we must trust
that it grows,
and allow others
to savour
its fruit.

No secrets =
No skeletons.

Being
impatient
is a waste
of time.

Before
we can be fully great,
we need to be
grate-full.*

Cursed
be ye
who concurs
my excuses
for me.

My quest
is not to do my job;
my quest
is to do my work.

Fog
is always thicker
from a distance.

You
never know
who has the answer
to your
questions
until you ask.

When you realize
that you need a light
in your life,
why look
for a lamp?

The only
time
"head"
should precede
"heart"
is in
the dictionary.

Treasures
are rarely discovered
on the well-worn
path.

A puppet
is a puppet,
no matter how long
the strings are.

The eyes
reveal
what
the lips
conceal.

In the end
we accomplish nothing,
except
what we became.

Even the mighty eagle
must first flap its wings
if it wishes to soar.

How can
you inspire
if you have never
perspired?

Sometimes
in order to
see clearly,
we need to
close our
eyes.

In life
there is no "fail-safe,"
so it is helpful
to have a place
to fail safely.

In my heart,
I am free;
it is the mind,
that tricks me.

All money
is borrowed.
How much interest
are you
willing to pay?

To those who say
that the "world" is dangerous
- I would suggest that
the "word" is more so.

Today
is just an ordinary day,
perfect
in every way.

Evolution
is simply
perfection
in motion.

A home built out of
material
will not last a lifetime;
a home built out of
love
will last an eternity.

If thou
wishest to be free,
Death
thine friend
first must be.

Every sunset
is also a sunrise;
it all depends
on where
you stand.

The difference
between a
lonely life
and a
lovely life
is nv.

Wake,
and be aware
of your wake,
before your wake.

The dreams
we abandon
become the ghosts
that haunt
our nightmares.

Do we actually
discover anything,
or do we merely
reveal it?

Hating
hate
truly is a
double negative.

Goals,
like flowers,
wilt quickly
once picked,
unless they receive
nurturing
and attention.

Gifts

can only be unwrapped

AFTER

they are received.

Many wait;
some create.

The Universe
starts with
U.

When you look
in the mirror
please be gentle...
for you are looking
into the eyes
of God.

Sometimes
the best way
for a person to learn
a lesson
is to give them
what they want.

Greed
is a weed
seed.

Consciousness =
the information
in the vibration.

When we are thinking,
we are
merely talking
to ourselves;
therefore,
shouldn't we watch
what we say?

The Past
is a comfortable blanket
in which one shrouds oneself
during moments of despair,
yet it quickly becomes
a sarcophagus
that tightens
and constricts
and chokes away
all of our air.

At what point
does noise
become music?

More treasure
can come from
a gold mind
than a gold mine.

For now,
enjoy this,
and when
this
is no longer,
enjoy that.

As we attempt
to understand the essence
of the universe using
only the rational mind,
we will never
understand "why"
and forever shall
be to "how" confined.

There never was,
and never will be,
another person
like you or me,
so in the end
we can disagree,
but please let's do so
peacefully.

The fact
that you are here is,
in itself,
proof that
you have faith.

If a destination
cannot exist
without a journey,
but a journey
can exist
without a destination,
then where does
the power lie?

E – nergy

G – iven

O - ut

Goal - within it
lies the means of
achieving it:
first you have to
get up and
GO,
then you have to
continue
AL (L)
the way.

My choice
is to not suffer
in disbelief.

The trick
to getting
somewhere/something
quickly is simple:
don't be in a hurry!

The difference between
arrogance
and
confidence
lies in who you're
trying to
convince.

We are all
just renting.

Garage Sale
- today or
tomorrow -
your choice

Everything
that gets done
is started
by a force of
one.

Once a skeptic,
always
a skeptic. =;0)

History:
one person's opinion
of the past.

When we pray,
to the universe we say,
"I want it my way,"
but when we meditate,
our thoughts germinate,
and only then do we
become
truly great.

Some people
collect pity points
as a type of currency
that they use
to pay for
emotional debt.

Busy bee-ing
or
busy being?

"Someday"
is
the day after
tomorrow.

Whether willing or not,
motion is inherent;
everything changes and
movement is a permanent
and integral part of the system.
Of course,
we always have "choice":
to move willingly,
or be pushed.

If you
"think"
you love someone,
you don't.

When it's answers
that you seek,
listen,
rather than speak.

When it comes
to success,
it is important
to surround yourself
with cheerleaders,
not fear breeders.

Perfection
is in
perception.

Take heed;
even the
most bitter
of poisons
is easy to swallow
when coated
with honey.

The only thing
interfering with my ability
to become non-judgmental
is the behavior
of the morons
and jerks of the world. =;0)

You
or
ewe?

While others
can provide the spark,
only we can
fuel the flame.

Giving up your
beliefs and values
is usually erosion
more so
than explosion.

It's good to live
in the moment,
and even better
to love
in the moment.

F-uture

E-vents

A-ppearing

R-eal

Let your actions
ripple through eternity
on wings of truth.

The road less traveled
is usually the one
not paved.

◇ BUMP ◇

Satori:

at-one-ment

in a moment.

A key component
of mental fitness
is to
work out the doubt.

It doesn't matter
how loud
opportunity knocks
if the occupant
is out to lunch.

I'm striving
to be indifferent
to our differences.

Being patient
doesn't mean
being passive.

Perhaps we can't control
the direction of the wind;
however, only the foolhardy
would take their hands
off of the rudder.

If people are
no longer interested in your
"feel-sorry" story,
perhaps it is because
they have already heard
the ending too many times.

Competition
comes from common goals;
connectivity comes from
common questions.

Perhaps
the reason
we are born
with two eyes and
two ears
is to remind us
to see and hear
both sides.

The things I see,
when I see,
the God that is me.

Often
the most powerful thing
we can say
comes not
from the spoken word.

Every second,
and every minute,
has inspiration
and magic in it.

Ideas and insights
are impotent
without
implementation.

One little spark,
A tiny light,
Illuminates the dark,
Vanishes the night.

What doesn't kill you
makes for
an interesting book.

The key to a delicious life
is to enjoy
the last bite
as much as the first.

If we wait
for our critics
to be silent
before we sing,
we will be forever mute.

Destiny is the canvas
that you have been given;
free-will is
the palette and brush
that you colour it with.

I am only responsible
for that which I can control.

Thoughts matter
and become matter.

When I stop growing,
I know
that I'll
be going.

Cyber-homes for some amazing people

I believe that there are a great number of people and organizations who are helping to improve the quality of other people's journey and who are making their wisdom available via the Internet. This list is by no means complete and **I am in no way trying to give the impression that the people on this list are endorsing my work** (other than those explicitly quoted in the testimonials section), these are just people whose work I admire, or with whom I have had conscious contact. By "conscious contact" I mean that I have had a direct personal experience with these individuals and I whole-heartedly support the message that they are conveying. While I know that there are numerous other individuals out there doing similar work, or other inspiring work, I do not feel it is appropriate to add a connection to a person or to an organization with whom I am unfamiliar. Due to the physical nature of this book, the information on this list is current as of the print date; however, the information may be outdated by the time you read this, so I will make updates to the list on my website: **www.TinyThoughtGuy.com** as frequently as possible.

Adam McLeod: www.dreamhealer.com

Alan Cohen: www.alancohen.com

Anthony de Mello:
www.demellospirituality.com

Barbara Marx Hubbard:
www.barbaramarxhubbard.com

Bernie Siegel: www.berniesiegelmd.com

Bob Proctor:
www.proctorgallagherinstitute.com

Brian Swimme
www.storyoftheuniverse.org

Byron Katie: www.byronkatie.com

Carl Hammerschlag: www.healingdoc.com

Caroline Leaf: www.drleaf.com

Cynthia Sue Larson:
www.realityshifters.com

Dalai Lama: www.dalailama.com

Dan Millman: www.peacefulwarrior.com

David Carson: www.medicinecards.com

David Hamilton: www.drdavidhamilton.com

David Suzuki: www.davidsuzuki.org

Deepak Chopra: www.deepakchopra.com

Denis Waitley: www.waitley.com

Desmond Tutu: www.tutu.org

Edgar Cayce: www.edgarcayce.org

Fred Alan Wolf: www.fredalanwolf.com

Gary Zukav: www.seatofthesoul.com

Gregg Braden: www.greggbraden.com

Iyanla Vanzant:
www.innervisionsworldwide.com

Jack Kornfield: www.jackkornfield.com

James Van Praagh: www.vanpraagh.com

Jean Houston: www.jeanhouston.org

Joan Borysenko: www.joanborysenko.com

Joe Dispenza: www.drjoedispenza.com

Larry Dossey: www.dosseydossey.com

Lauren MacLauclan:
www.lawofattractiontrainingroom.com

Lynne McTaggart:
www.lynnemctaggart.com

Marc Allen: www.marcallen.com

Marilyn Schlitz: www.marilynschlitz.com

Meg Wheatley:
www.margaretwheatley.com

Nelson Mandela: www.nelsonmandela.org

Oprah Winfrey: www.oprah.com

Pam Grout: www.pamgrout.com

Patch Adams: www.patchadams.org

Paulo Coelho: www.paulocoelho.com

Pema Chodron:
www.pemachodronfoundation.org

Peter McWilliams: www.mcwilliams.com

Rhonda Byrne: www.rhondabyrne.net

Richard Bach: www.richardbach.com

Rosemary Altea: www.rosemaryaltea.com

Sanaya Roman: www.sanayaroman.com

Shakti Gawain: www.shaktigawain.com

Sounds True: www.soundstrue.com

Susan Jeffers: www.susanjeffers.com

Thich Nhat Hanh: www.plumvillage.org

Wayne Dyer: www.drwaynedyer.com

Subject matter experts

Dan Poynter: www.parapublishing.com

Jim Rohn: www.jimrohn.com

Lisa Nichols:
www.motivatingthemasses.com

Napoleon Hill: www.naphill.org

Steve Harrison: www.steveharrison.com

The Learner Within
www.thelearnerwithin.com

'Click to Donate' websites (free to you):

Care 2: www.care2.com

Greater Good: www.greatergood.com

Free Rice: www.freerice.com